Precipitates

⁂

Precipitates

Poems by
Debra Kang Dean

AMERICAN POETS CONTINUUM SERIES, NO. 81

BOA Editions, Ltd. ❧ Rochester, NY ❧ 2003

First Edition
03 04 05 06 7 6 5 4 3 2 1

Publications by BOA Editions, Ltd.—
a not-for-profit corporation under section 501 (c) (3)
of the United States Internal Revenue Code—
are made possible with the assistance of grants from
the Literature Program of the New York State Council on the Arts,
the Literature Program of the National Endowment for the Arts,
the Sonia Raiziss Giop Charitable Foundation,
the Lannan Foundation,
as well as from the Mary S. Mulligan Charitable Trust,
the County of Monroe, NY,
Ames-Amzalak Memorial Trust,
and The CIRE Foundation.

See Colophon on page 96 for special individual acknowledgments.

Cover Design: Lisa Mauro/Mauro Design
Cover Photograph: "Fall Leaves Afloat, near Beech Spring" by Scot Miller, courtesy of the
    photographer.
Interior Design and Composition: Richard Foerster
Manufacturing: McNaughton & Gunn, Lithographers
BOA Logo: Mirko

Library of Congress Cataloging-in-Publication Data

Dean, Debra Kang, 1955–
    Precipitates / Debra Kang Dean.
        p. cm. — (American poets continuum series, v. 81)
    ISBN 1–929918–43–7 (pbk. : alk. paper)
        I. Title. II. Series.

PS3554.E154P74 2003
811'.54—dc22

2003058253

BOA Editions, Ltd.
Thom Ward, Editor
H. Allen Spencer, Chair
A. Poulin, Jr., President & Founder (1938–1996)
260 East Avenue, Rochester, NY 14604
www.boaeditions.org

Even in Kyoto—
hearing the cuckoo's cry—
I long for Kyoto.

—Bashō

❈

I would drink deeper; fish in the sky,
whose bottom is pebbly with stars.

—Thoreau

Contents

Precipitates

Weather Report

Fifteen miles west of Boston
and mostly the news is of small creatures
and snow. A self-appointed snow inspector,
I tune in to the weather: snow and sun,
sometimes clouds or showers or wind
or chattering letters that spell *chilly*.
As with everywhere I've lived
the forecasters look like
Vanna White surrogates or
used-car salesmen. Still,
they grow on you
like poker pals upping the ante—
with shifts of pressure.
Sometimes the weather calls their bluff.
Still, they, at least, seem to know
where they are. Right now
a light snow is falling,
a steady downpour
of flakes fine as gnats.
To her usual, "What's up?"
I give my old friend the usual answer:
"Same old shit shoveled a different way."
I bundle up. Before I thread my fingers
through the shovel's handle,
it flashes a conspiratorial grin.

Patchwork of Selvage

(January–April 1999)

i.

Snow. A few red pines
edging the lawn outside this
window's forty panes—

in a white world, they harbor
islands still green where they stand

between earth's blank slate
and the slate-gray sky. Aging
is like this: whittled

down by gusts, fallen away
all dead wood, what's left bends then

rights itself even
under the burden of snow,
winter's argument.

Late afternoon's pitched lub-dub
of geese veeing their way east

punctuates silence
and turns our gaze away from
the dawning sunset,

each, now, spelling the lengthening
of days. The sky answers

in orange, coral,
then pale indigo crosshatched
with sixteen black crows.

In a small room like this one,
scented by woodsmoke and perfume,

a woman unsets
one place setting, untouched, then
washes her dishes

and gives herself instead to
blue-green lines in a blank book.

First nothing, lines con-
fine like bars; then cramped figures
walking a tightrope,

then, as if she had entered
a pool, sleek letters, weightless

now, and now every-
thing still but the one hand's sure
return at line's end.

There, here on the page, three lines
intersect: then, now, and then.

Have a cup of tea.
It is that simple. Only
tend to the making—

temperature is everything,
as with snow's grains, beads, flecks, flakes—

the exact green shade
seen once and forever known
in tea steeped dark, light.

Light. *Drink and be whole beyond
confusion* written in frost

thawing on the panes.
So, sun up, sun down, each day,
a small rehearsal

of faith. Not words but in the vast
unknowing, one thing known:

some new thing will catch
in the fragile nets we weave
before it slips through,

though the child's delight
is in touch, taste. "See," he points,

sloshing around in
galoshes. Of no use to
anyone, he grows.

Among the barren branches,
the bittersweet's berries light.

Inside, they will blow
on thick soup steaming in bowls
his mother's hands made.

Holding one, its warmth, she feels
her teacher's hands guide her hands.

Her child, she knows, is
clay in her hands, whose center
she will lightly pull

or push against to raise him
till he comes into his own.

Too soon the impress
of angels they left outside
these forty panes, gone.

ii.

The swish of a broom
against the walk even here,
hear it? And one bird,

puffed up against a stiff wind,
the lean cat, before it lifts.

Meanwhile, as cats go,
this one's simply passing through—
and couldn't care less,

as at eye level, last seeds
of a milkweed pull free.

At a safe distance
above them both, one crow rubs
its beak on a branch.

Forty-four degrees at noon:
a mosquito hovering.

Even the baffle
can't stop the squirrel from shaking
free sunflower seeds.

A black sun on thawing snow
herringboned by mourning doves.

And one man who'd left
open every door—what for?—
shuts them one by one.

Another day. The sun's slight
northwesterly arc towards spring.

One dog, unleashed, zig-
zags down a private road, sniffs,
lifts its leg, trots on.

And today, drizzle, some rain.
Good thing, this umbrella, till

it's seized by the wind
which exposes its stiff give—
empty turtle shell.

In the clearing's surrounding
pines, the wind inhales, exhales.

On this narrow road
meandering uphill, step
around fallen limbs.

Not even its paved surface
can deflect this weathering,

and so it's for us
to learn the language of sky,
to look at road kill.

Water wavers on the shore-
line of the frozen pond.

In the fog of sleep,
a picture window gazed through
appears, disappears

and is supplanted by three
daffodils on a nightstand.

She loves lingering
in bed, long beyond the early
fleeting half-light

on a cold Sunday morning—
crisp room, the smell of coffee.

Mercury falling.
The news for tomorrow is
snow. Goodbye, clear sky!

One shovelful at a time,
and a path opens ahead.

Easy to see flecks
turning into sticky flakes
and know the meaning.

Lunch: a little miso soup
with tofu and wakame

while outside, the cat
waits for the door to open
a crack to slip through,

having laid tangles of tracks
vanishing into the woods.

iii.

For the moment, two
blue jays have ceased to shatter
the air with their shrieks.

Sometimes silence oppresses
like the humid summer air.

Only disconnect,
and each thing becoming it-
self becomes nothing

before rain on the flashing
slurs into the same dull speech.

A delivery truck,
gears slipping and grinding up
the hill, not yet here.

From the mouth of the hose un-
coiled, water cutting a course;

it evaporates.
Two days later, it's snowing
again. Bitter cold.

Like whipped cream, snow on the perch—
a junco's the first to feed.

The clack of antlers—
no, only wind in the trees,
snow falling in bursts;

before nightfall, one lamp lights
snow wind broadcasts from the roof.

All night such music
from a simple set of chimes
on a sheltered tree.

This brass lamp smudged, dulled by touch—
but polished, see how it shines!

Just off the trail up
Pine Hill, three snowballs stacked like
mochi, tangerines—

and faintly the scent of pipe-
smoke, almost a voice humming.

Snow falls, weighs on bare
branches, pine boughs, it falls
and the ground grows white.

Geese still cross this sky unheard,
gone, gone, to another shore.

The cloudless sky says
nothing of what's beyond it,
sighs, *This, only this.*

The expanse of blue darkens
then clears again. Just ride it.

Bumpy ascent through
a haze of clouds—above it
an infinite blue—

bound earthward. Mud sucked at heels
under the eerie revving

of three blades of one
windmill on a windmill farm
in Minnesota,

where the deep rich soil smells still
of still water, fields swept clear.

Old leaves scrape against
the pavement here in Lincoln,
Massachusetts. Home

on the vernal equinox,
we left the prairie, waving.

Alarm clocks turned off
before they sound. A sign, yes,
marking the season

of boot prints snaking along
crisp paths—cockleburs, deer ticks,

and the crocuses'
snow-white blooms. Among tousled
dead leaves, their green leaves.

Two cardinals—one present,
one absent—sing in that tree.

Flowing water feels
this point of confluence, this
divergence and does,

seeking the lowest way, find
its own. "Make a little progress

every day," Master
Jou, Tsung Hwa, said—"Practice." What-
ever you feel, you do.

iv.

Seventy degrees—
fish, unseen, etching the sur-
face of Walden Pond

as daily now, more day dawns.
Desire—a stone's throw away.

Persistent knocking
off somewhere in the trees—one
nuthatch pauses here,

the wind not quite a whisper
amid birdsong, mosquitoes.

How far have we come?
This pipestone turtle: RL
sealed it with beeswax

but he who quarried the stone
from hard rock remains unnamed.

For weeks, feeding on
insects, unnoticed—robins
calling from the trees.

Island on island, a lone
turtle sunning in the pond.

Drawing back curtains
from four windows at first light:
whole worlds—in this one.

Far off, as if from dreams, comes
the drone of planes—or are they

boats clouding the blue
waters? Time stills them. Distilled,
the thing seen is seen.

Bashō sees through touch; touch him
anywhere, and he'll read you.

Water runs through the hand
tensed open or closed, but cupped
the hand holds; it pools.

One pedestrian weaving
between the cars—no false steps.

A desk's four corners:
beyond the reach of cool sun-
light falling without

on the cat wandering free
and easy, dirt drenched, rolling.

What safe place is there?
The fruit of the peach palm, hearts
of palm, dead center.

No clouds. Weathercock, robins,
clouds of ten thousand insects

rising from moist earth,
stagnant pools, from rotted wood—
they glisten and sing.

Spring peepers, crickets to come,
and one voice, lit like incense,

sings "Amazing Grace"
amid grief sounds caught in the
throats of survivors.

In the Everglades, full-throated
fire roars its one sure note.

Helpless against wind
and sun, reading the sky, they
look on, wait for rain.

Chapel Hill's dogwoods unfurl
their pale pink blossoms, waving.

A five-pointed star,
he stands, fingers tingling, crown point
and feet strung taut . . .

Between heaven and earth, what
we've always craved is water.

Coloring our hands,
refracted light can't be held,
and so we look on.

Twitching at noon—what strange dream
rouses the cat from its nap?

Already its pupils
begin to contract, round eyes
bright, sunlit mirrors.

Gaze into them long enough
they begin to give you back.

Heart Sutras

Hail

I was eleven the first time I saw it,
the November afternoon gone
heavy and gray. I'd begun
to doze when something—
not palm fronds rustling
nor monkey pods rattling,
but more like spoons against glass
or small bells—something began
clinking against the second story's
blue palings and rails, lightly at first,
bringing all of us, even the teacher,
to our feet and out the door.

                                Not since,
three years before, when the staticky
Standard Oil broadcast had been
interrupted by news that brought to tears
even Miss Engard (who didn't tax
our imaginations too hard playing
the part of witch at Halloween)
had there been so much commotion.
Seeing our teachers openly weeping
had frightened us even more than a word
like *assassination*.

                      Above us,
concrete. Under our feet, concrete.
And all of us stretching our hands
beyond the blue rails to catch,
as they fell, clear pieces of sky
that burned a second,
melting in our hands.

The Eulogy

Roughly the size of a grain of rice,
the scar is barely visible now. Touching it
brings back my mother's mouth saying

nothing before I left that evening
and my sister's saying "lemon juice"
when I returned. She was up,

not waiting, watching TV.
I sliced a lemon and rubbed its juice
into the ink stamped on my hand at the first

of a string of bars. Fifteen years gone, I'd been
more guest than family tagging along with cousins—
my first time ever bar-hopping in Honolulu.

Unwilling to offend with my "good English,"
I'd mostly listened, nodded and sipped as they drank,
and we made small talk and made our money talk,

one-upping each other by flashing bills
for the next round. At the Korcan bar,
when conversation flagged, we sang karaoke.

Half of me wishes I'd gotten wasted with them.
And the part of me struggling to stay awake wonders
what made me say yes in the first place.

At the kitchen sink, I'd traded lemon juice first for soap,
then for soap and the light scraping of my thumbnail,
then thumbnail and running water, then soap

and a nylon scouring pad. Afterwards,
with my sister, I sat in the dark till the movie ended.
The next morning I dressed for the funeral, where

because not one among the 500 gathered could speak
as a friend, on behalf of the family, my mother
had asked me to speak. And simply because I could

I spoke of my grandmother's life and read a few poems.
The spot I'd rubbed raw glistened and stung
like flesh under a freshly broken blister.

Soap

My husband, already undressed,
sets three two-foot lengths of logs

in the river, while our four-year-old
tosses stone after stone from the shore

and I finish undressing. I wince
as I step into the river.

Sitting on the coarse cut-end
of a log, I lift one foot

then the other, into
and out of the water,

which has begun to make red
socks of my husband's feet.

When I call him, my son chooses to stand
knee deep in the river, so I lather my hands

then wash my arms, my breasts
as he mirrors my motions.

Passing the soap among us,
we work down to our feet.

When my son's teeth start to chatter,
my husband and I make bowls of our hands

and help him to rinse.
His body stiffens.

A quick nod, and he's on the shore,
cupping himself with both hands

as if against the grazing cows
that have lifted their heads.

This is the last time he will see me naked.

✦

Customs

Barely out of Greenville, North
Carolina, three cars plug along
ahead of you on the two-lane
no-passing-zone stretch of farm road,
and you, white-knuckled, behind again,
casting ahead to your destination
two-and-a-half hours away. The truth is
they are doing fifty-five
in a fifty-five zone. So you turn
on the radio to "chill"
as your son likes to tell you,
which slowly turns you all inside.
So you don't take note of how
one by one the cars ahead of you begin
pulling off the road. Instead,
in front of you, you see a clear lane
and a line of cars, headlights on,
proceeding past you. It's like this
when you glance the customs of a place
you will always be new to;
even after eight years, there's
some surprise to knock you out
of cruise control. You find yourself
in the middle of it, whatever it is,
embarrassed by your own uncouth.
Funeral. Somebody taking up
permanent residence. It registers
after you've accelerated past
the first pulled-over car and
the second one, where you manage finally
to yield. It's why, up north
in your new apartment a year later,
Elizabeth, a friend's daughter not yet two,
who's spent two weeks on the road

in a rented car, will touch you: when she turns
away from you to point to nowhere
in particular that you can gather
and says to her mother, "Home, home,"
you will feel what she means.

Kyrielle

Perched on the blue spruce, one crow,
blue-black, eyeing the expanse of yard,
is taking inventory. Below,
one squirrel, one woodchuck, one bluebird.

Today, perhaps, it's the simple
act of counting that serves as reward;
its toes clench as it sinks on its heels:
There's one squirrel, one woodchuck, one bluebird.

Refuse it the solid ground of
your open hand, Chien Hou discovered,
and a sparrow can't take flight, unlike the
one squirrel, one woodchuck, one bluebird.

I stand by a third-floor window
days and days, saying not one word,
opaque and shrunken, like noonday's shadow
of one squirrel, one woodchuck, one bluebird.

Strays

To scoop clumps of piss
and chunks out of the litterbox
long after my son has grown
out of diapers is humbling.

These cats—to have them
was his idea, a promise
he, at thirteen, held me
to make good on.

And when he left last year
they were mine, all mine.
When he calls, we talk music
and higher math, but no talk yet

of the time when, out of old
grievances I hadn't resolved,
it was him I struck. He carries
my darkness in him. And yet,

what prescient wisdom
led him to leave me these cats
to tether me to a world
I might too easily forsake,

to practice, daily, tenderness?
Yesterday, a stray stood outside
our wrought-iron back gate,
sniffing the air as I ate.

Behind the door behind me
my cats eyed it. The stray
stepped through the gate,
stopped, stepped slowly

toward me. I wanted
to call it in. I'm sure hunger
would have led it, surely
as even now some nights

the long road calls and calls.
The stray took slow steps.
Behind me my cats
growled and hissed. I wanted

to call it in. I stood,
instead, clapping my hands
and hissing to drive it off. Inside,
Bashō and Cricket relaxed.

Arrival

*One will have followed the rules in the human
stage when the practice of Tai-Chi Chuan
outdoors does not disturb flocks of birds.*
 —Jou, Tsung Hwa

I was in deep, through
Grasp Bird's Tail and Single Whip,
the occasional scrape of unswept leaves underfoot
on the patio brick become a part of the motion,
when it appeared first in the sycamore,
then on the eaves, on the rim of the birdbath
I'd filled only the day before, then back
to the sycamore, but because, as I said,
I was in deep, through Lifting Hands
and White Crane Cools Its Wings,
at first I saw only the flicker of another
gray bird that finally perched on the eaves
leaning and leaning, turning its eye this way,
this way, until it caught my eye,
its gesture turning my mind to Twain's
"Baker's Bluejay Yarn" for a moment, and there I was,
about to laugh at the bird, whose painted eye
gave it away, when it lifted above the roof, disappeared,
but as I was about to go on to Hug Knee Left
and down to Needle at the Sea Bottom,
to the well of Cloud Hands, twelve
cedar waxwings ringed the bath, dipping
and dipping to fill their beaks, unceasingly
chattering, filling the silence, stilling my hands
first at my sides, then slipping them up under my armpits
because it was February and cool,
and though I knew in stopping I'd passed
on the chance to take the test that spells arrival,
for the first time in a long time

I was out there, watchful and still
until they returned to the nowhere
out of which they came.

"Crazy"

in memory of Patsy Collier

No one I know had quite
perfected that typically Southern
greeting the way you did,

giving the diphthong a stretch
each time you said it, almost turning
the word polysyllabic. Hearing you

say it, I always thought of that other Patsy
singing "Crazy," which is how I felt
each day rising my first year

in North Carolina's coastal plains, my eyes
suffering some strain of phantom pain
at the absence of mountains. A whole year.

And then one day I was seeing
clear again to the crazed displays
of lightning and sunsets.

And then two years ago
you began wearing to the office
a blue caftan, and I was back,

each time I saw you in it, home
for a day; it was Aloha Friday.
So how can I say we live in one place?

When my husband had his
heart attack last September,
I was on my way back from

Bodega Bay, the friends I'd left
fast returning to memory,
where my dead live. Where my husband

could have but didn't take up
permanent residence. Gone that way
are the spirit masters you showed me

how to use that first year. Holding the botched
fourth, I said, "I need a new one."
Thought, having already torn up three, *I need it*

to be perfect. A slight parting
and tensing of lips, a lifting of brows,
you saying, "Here, let me see it,"

and taking it from my hand.
Turning the white sheet over,
from its underside you scraped

with a razor blade (*semper paratus*)
the raised blue error, whose letters had almost
gone square from overstrike. Then flipping

the sheet back down and, for my sake,
dabbing then blowing the liquid
paper dry, you said, "There,

now, you can fix it."

Taproot

Stooping to pull up a weed,
I think of my father
who made of weeding an art.

After work, he'd take a bucket
and his weeder from the toolshed
and clear an area of a yard he knew

would never look manicured,
whose quality would, at best,
be like something homemade.

He'd set the bucket upside down
and sit on it. Plotting a route
he'd shift the bucket, a move

so deft you might think he was just
leaning out to extend his reach.
He knew exactly where and what angle

to drive the weeder down,
north and south of the weed,
without severing its taproot.

When my father worked like this,
making small mounds he'd later
gather up in his bucket,

the dog would sniff at his bare feet
then lie down in the shade his body made.
Grounded there, he was most himself,

his hunger for perfection and control
giving way, finally, to the work itself.
It was easy to love him then.

❧

Ordinary Moons

i.

At bedtime the child says, "Father,
Tell me a story." The father calls on Q-tips, a bar
Of soap, spiders, water gurgling, and so on.

ii.

In the living room, the wife draws a light bulb out of the heel
Of a sock, then with her darning needle weaves
To lock the thread. She takes a shirt from her basket to sew on

iii.

A button. "Do me a favor," she says, as the husband
Enters the room. "Hand me the blue thread."
In their bed, they hug, kiss, and so on.

iv.

"How like the eye of a needle you sometimes are,"
She says. And he: "You defy fingering. You are
A panpipe, or Jupiter's moons, or maybe . . ." And so on.

v.

Tomorrow's full moon is the numbered button
God lights with His finger, a sign
The almanac tells them to sow on.

vi.

In a month, the seeds will have sprouted.
They'll work in the garden, burying fish heads,
Weeding, thinning, mulching, and so on.

vii.

A story, Twain said, is "one damn thing
After another." But life?—life is only one thing. In full sun
A writer pares, like nails or apple skin, and-so-ons.

Adam's Apple

i.

At twenty months my nephew,
having already mastered the sound
of sense, held my attention
as I sliced an apple crosswise
to show him the stars.

After he'd strung three pieces
on his finger then tossed them
on the floor, he shrieked
and kicked and pointed
an insistent finger

elsewhere. Like *the dunce*
who searched for fire
with a lighted lantern, "Tell me,"
I pleaded, "tell me"
you little Neanderthal.

ii.

The skeleton found at Kebara
made me rethink *Neanderthal.*

Among the remains a hyoid—
shaped like a wishbone almost

the length of my thumb. Bone?
I press thumb and index finger

against my throat in search
of my own hyoid bone.

The 60,000 years between us contract:
He *could* speak. And I—

there was a time I couldn't speak.
Some days, loving the lump in my throat

I think of the impulse to name
as Adam's curse, our apple.

iii.

Not the ash, but the bones
are the reason we cremate;
picking through what remains

with chopsticks, we're after
this one, in particular,
Arimoto insists, pointing

at his Adam's apple—
we burn off the flesh,
he says, and fire the bones

just till they break
under their own weight—
nodobotoke, we call it

Buddha in the throat.

Patchwork of Selvage

(May–August 1999)

v.

Always the first step
is preparation—a line
drawn between two worlds.

As if air were water, thin
currents lifting strands of hair.

The hard bud of one
peony unpacks itself—
empties its center.

Jonquils fling back the cold rain
steadily falling all day

while, in Missoula,
death reveals the shapeliness
of one good man's life:

see? in the poems she will write
one clear mind's full flowering.

A coin struck by light
blinds through its hard brilliance. But
held, the coin grows warm.

A leash tethers master and
dog; no small feat keeping it slack!

It was touch and go
winter long for the fall-planted
dogwood now in bloom.

Sure as yesterday's rain, we'd
seen it coming—and yet . . .

Not a disaster
exactly, this killing frost—
some petals, brown-edged.

The new moon's rising—dark face
hidden among blinking stars.

Between two black urns,
thin stems of three narcissi
held by a blue vase.

Sound on the TV turned down—
easy to read their faces.

In the Pintlar Range
a cow stops on a two-lane
near the broken fence.

Eyes deadlocked one long moment—
a few flakes of snow falling

as in Billings, framed
by rimrock, the cottonwoods
shed their snow-white fluff.

At dawn, Walden's surface breached
by a lone swimmer rising.

In this place Rinzai
tells us to carry on the same
tasks—wake, eat, talk, sleep.

Somewhere someone is pulling
shut a door for the last time.

Like magnets turned north
to north, father and son clear
a space between them.

Scars—where insects bit, burn from
a woodstove, blisters on heels.

Sun speckled under
red pines, he drowses, leaving
the world to its wake.

Cat's eyes trained on the robin, oh!
Sad is it, or beautiful?

Words, words, words—only
wind filling a few dresses
hanging out to dry.

From Makamachekamuck,
Mt. Monadnock, Wachusett.

That man now peddling
his bicycle up the hill—
Bashō thinks, *A mouse?*

After a week of rain, out
come soap, buckets, hoses, spades.

On a day like this
one, sunlight falls even on
the unbelievers.

Bearing the peacepipe, he turned
to face the four directions,

what is above and
what is below. Better to
walk the line than choose.

vi.

Leaving the lights on
the screen, we stepped out into
another dark place.

Slow lift off for the blue jay—
mouse, a large bean, still squeaking.

No small task shucking
the husk, chewing steamed kernels
clean down to the cob.

The dogs, too, so full, they sprawl,
will raise only an eyebrow.

Grains of pollen sift
through the open windows' screens
borne by, *with* the wind.

This is the best time, seeing
through the clarifying dark

to the no, and al-
so to the yes in this state
of transformation—

because listening is one
kind of seeing. She jots notes:

for each cup a tea-
spoon plus one more for the pot—
to acknowledge it.

No describing the bitter-
sweetness once it's passed the lips—

one sits waist deep in
the Pacific, half in, half
out of one's element.

A squirrel hotfoots it along
black lines to reach a feeder

hung high under eaves
on the shady side, barely
swinging this way, that.

In small increments the wood-
chuck sheds the guise of pine bark;

now in the open
he cuts a path up into
the flower garden.

In entering bring your own
tea, wine, whatever you choose.

Hailing the pale hues
of summer-yet-to-come, pines
shake loose their spent cones.

For now, highbush blueberries
turning a filmy deep blue.

To catch the eye of
the mailman, a slip of red
raised like a child's arm.

Each measured step back up toward
the house—one way of praying.

The short night—a tale
of bonfires in Spain, pepper
on corn like ashes.

Eating, piecemeal we're being
eaten. How much is enough?

Rain might keep falling
into this hollow; the soil
would keep taking it.

Seeing no one thing but all
things on the edge—that's the trick.

What the river knows,
restless, attaching itself
nowhere, *flowing, flown*.

In the gas stove's blue-tipped flame
Prometheus still winces.

How preserve the child's
innocent question fingering
the unknown, "What's this?"

Feeling the stick's heft, weighing
word against deed: *strike, stricken*.

Against the table's
light shellac coat, big rain drops
bounce and slide and bead

and turn us inside, nightfall
a curtain after last call.

vii.

When, finally, rain
falls inch deep, asphalt hisses,
steams, then there's runoff.

Set on a desk, the spirit
level's bubble settles true.

Air hazy from heat
and humidity—leaves slouch,
showing their pale backs.

One stick of incense burning
steadily down to the quick.

Out from the rod's tip
a single line, weighted, arcs,
sinks, and is drawn back.

A brown bat, caught inside, loops
figure eights, seeks an escape—

the cat makes a pass
at it, catches it, and you
step in, release it.

A man in a green hammock
might almost merge with the trees,

while another rides
the current midstream, feeling
his way down river,

and another spends all day
tending his nine rows of beans.

Spiraling out of
one fixed point, each imperfectly
mirroring each—

these gyroscopes tottering
reflect light as best they can.

What passed here—unseen
till, finding the scent, one dog
starts fleshing it out.

Bumblebees lost in windfall
sunflowers sprung from birdseed.

Their wrists dipped and turned—
he, tasseled sword sheathed, gazing
at her clean brush strokes.

They say in the hazy dark,
one must trust the instruments.

In this year of drought,
some lawns, sun-bleached as towheads,
will outlive the trees.

Scattered petals—*what falls a-*
way is always. And is near.

For today, at least,
when rain snaps the string of heat
birds walk, still themselves—

reporting, a familiar
voice wavers, catches, then holds.

Divers' air bubbles
rising from the ocean floor—they
do not hold their breath.

Barely visible, bullfrogs
on the pond's shore—watch out flies!

Today, idleness—
sanding smooth a stick's cut ends
under the cool pines.

Floating on a thin layer
of tears—cut pieces of glass.

Rain dissolving one
snail's trail ascending the wall—
who remembers it?

Or the first slippery green shapes,
like thoughts, rising from the sea.

Darkness will translate
the owl's hard labor into
the mind's pure gesture

while in basements traps will spring
on the necks of baited mice.

When she found herself
taking the same easy path
again, she changed course.

When the still pond beheld her,
she recognized her true self

for an instant, before
rain dispersed her form into
fragments, both dark and light.

viii.

Beneath her, the land,
parsed by farmers, seemed endless
as the sea she'd left.

At home, zucchini ripen.
Daily from five hens, five eggs.

Rain splashed on the last
few bites as they headed in
to sunset—lightning.

And in the rustling of leaves
the sound of the ocean's surges.

Detain her, one said,
and the other one, word poor,
did—by tripping her.

The whole time we knew ourselves
as guests, the house never ours.

When the cat wounded
a butterfly, you broke its body
calmly, to free it.

How stiff its limb, how cold to
touch was the body she left.

Hours on end the wind
sounding the trees, the chimes, some-
one thinking nothing,

singing, "Tomato, tomahto,
Let's call the whole thing off."

Wearied by proffered
dei ex machina worn thin
as the bland wafers,

she simply waited for rain—
the smell, the sound as it fell

and, in the dark, watched
instead the Perseid showers
streak across the sky.

To the cat's insistent cry,
each morning, food, fresh water.

Some mornings, a goldfinch
at the feeder, a hawk's shrieks
and the hands forget—

busybodies, oh, strayed bees,
She of the Bee Light: *'tis thee.*

Back to the scratchwork,
no, the patchwork of selvage
from the day's remains.

"This piece," says her mother, "try
turning it a half turn, see

if it will fit here—"
a bench appears, and with it
a clearing, shade trees.

Straw hat tipped, she loafs—her book
nearby, a grounded butterfly:

eyes closed, useless as
the gnarled tree risen above her,
she's free to wander.

Lines cast, like a flyfisher's
or a spider's. To catch on.

Under the buzz and
glare of fluorescent lights, hands
cradle tense jaws.

Who'd want, squat like a toad on
the throne, to face a mirror?

On my 65ᵗʰ
b-day / I kissed her, WC
W wrote, *while she pissed.*

There and not there, the valves of
her attention, opening.

Eyes pressed shut, seeking
cover, having fallen from
its nest—a lost squirrel.

Grass slick with morning's dense mist
headlights tunnel their way through.

The earth turning on
its axis moves as we move—
the same but different.

Rising, different but the same,
the sun, the day's first cordial,

belies the grammar
of distances that open
and close between us.

Traces

i. reflected light

On a two-lane, near the shoulder, bracing
itself against speed, a turtle's green face that is my face.

At the heart of the desert, an oasis
amid fasting and prayer. Lean face that is my face,

though I hunger, I am singing these praises
that rise like incense. A serene face, that is my face.

Not to the swift goes the race; time flies—and erases,
says the moon, sweet face that is my face.

I am walking into the dark woods' embrace
by a reflected light. Unseen face, that is my fate.

ii. *suspended*

By chance,
    a pine cone small as this pencil's eraser
was caught by a spider's invisible thread.
                            It was air-
borne,
    just above eye level, tottering a little
in the least breeze.

        Often I stitched the air
with my hand,
            windblown hair stroking
a black dog in the back seat,
                        sniffing the air.

When the fortune teller touched
                        my wrist, "Your life,"
she said in a foreign accent,
                "it's in the air?"
True to my birth sign, I let myself be pushed
into the train. Standing on tiptoe,
                    not quite all there.

⁕

iii. in jest

"Chunkectomy, more like—or divot—"
what I'd say if you asked. The name I give it
alone is windsock, empty seat. Not over but near enough
my heart. When the bandage came off, I gave it
a little feel. Thumbprint, shallow pool, in bad light
a cinnamon badge to remind me what I'm made of. I give it
a rest when it groans as I do, hearing the punch line
of a British friend's bad joke. I mean, he gives it
such brief space: "What's gray and comes
in buckets? An elephant," he says, "get it?"

iv. kudzu

In a plastic blue bowl half full of water
she's deposited Japanese beetles she found
on the roses. At dusk, I mistook them for glittery beads.

One wrong turn in North Carolina and I foundered,
lost in a maze of back roads in the land of kudzu.
The map is not the territory—held too dear, it becomes a foundry.

My sister and I encased the lower bunk with blankets and sheets.
We didn't know it was our own theater we were founding.
With flashlight, popsicle-stick puppets, Aesop's and Grimms' tales,

we built a world inside the small world we were drowning in.

v. two fishes

one fish breathless in air
                          when I saw
your heart's mitral valve
                  that's what I thought of

into a round red case my father re-coiling   the snake up from the pipe

static on the line
                    you repeating *what*   I thought of
how our words were being coded
                              then delivered as sound   the way

so often I hear and do not hear   at the same time   what I thought of
was mist still rising at first light
                  and the sun burning it off   what I thought of

then was not us but the old saw   *there is nothing new under the sun*

and woven head to tail two fishes
                        their eyes eclipse and moonrise
tonight the full moon seems
                  to have risen out of nowhere   as thoughts do

vi. wei

Say "I will" and "I do," and your will is done,
this once, words springing fullblown into action.

•

Before sighting down the rifle's barrel
a man I know tested the bolt's action.
No one wants to be caught hanging fire.

•

My son's favorite toy was part action-
figure, part timepiece. From a distance, undone,
it looked like a spider. He'd shout, "Action!"

•

I stand by. "Hmmm," I say, with delight
then a slight shudder—a typical reaction.

vii. tui shou

Late, as usual, I arrive, the last link

in the circle they're forming. We join hands
for a moment of silence. The scuba diver's wife drowned
alone in a pool. Time and chance. We form two lines, join wrists.

We repeat the drill. First, my line: "Metal ... Metal ... Metal ... Metal."

Then we respond from the other side: "...Water ... Wood ... Fire ... Earth."

We step left, bow, and, with another, join wrists.
Again. Again. "She is ash," he says, as we bow. We join wrists.
He's a grizzled bear of a man. Class ends. We bow.

"Mary," he says. He hugs me a long time, then lets go.

viii. empty hands

I've come with my two arms the one length—
but the genial hostess hands me a glass of wine.
At the wake,
            nobody knows my name.

But tonight there is no room for whining,
nor at the wedding, where we eat, drink, and
are merry. Look!
            My divorced parents are dancing. More wine!

One mad scientist, ecstatic, frisking around the table.
"It's alive, Igor," he's shouting, "it's alive!" Then he winds

down to tie up loose ends.
            Here is no bed of roses.
But now, while they last, we can catch, can ride the waves.

ix. for Emily

Shot from the cannon's mouth, here is my life
discharging the weapon. If I am still, the arc holds.
Better this than caged forever and thrashing the lion.
I stand on the fretwork of right triangles, where one line holds:
one-hundred-eighty degrees; plane to line, one-eighty

a pivot point, an about-face. Close up, the threshold
moment opens onto the taut traces lashing burden and beast.
Up to a point, subtraction undoes the vestige of every stronghold:
figure to plane, plane to line, line to point, down to
the one irrefutable point where we find ourselves beholden.

x. reprise

On a four-lane, skirting the breakdown, bracing
myself against the wheel—a possum's stunned face, that was my face.

In through a tangle of trees I followed a stream to the place
water gathers and flows. A glistening face, that was my face

though my heart was cheerful, too. I am whistling praises
through fear of this body's ashy leavings. A long face, that is my face.

Not to the swift goes the race, but tracing the arc of time's embrace,
says the sun on its course, *that sweet face is my face.*

I move through today's hard light of erasures
counting road kill. Unseen Face, that, too, is my face.

❧

Patchwork of Selvage
(September–December 1999)

ix.

Hurricane Dennis
churns the waters farther south.
At dusk, the first geese.

The burden of ripening
fruit weighing the vine earthward

—is that who you are,
hunched over under it? Trees
are groaning, *Let go*.

Squirrels chatter and squawk. Ghostly
the one mourning dove's five notes.

Under a growing
pile of letters, books, a bill
past due—too stuffy!

The sky's a soggy gray sponge
this morning, fog just lifting.

A seesaw, this sun-
shine, rain—and we are granted
one more day of summer.

Undoing studied designs—
these milkweeds and sunflowers.

Amused this ninth day
of the ninth month in the year
nineteen ninety-nine!

Umbrella hooked on her desk,
she's in the car. No break yet—

yellow leaves shaken
loose. On each one, veins forking
are paths on a path.

Out of the woods the woodchuck
up on two legs, looks ahead, back.

A crisp Granny Smith—
this morning's air chilling
a glass of orange juice.

Floyd's calm eye veering northwest
towards Florida—winds, big winds

now turning northeast—
spawning small tornadoes—whisk-
brooms near a vacuum.

Bridging the gap between chair
and sill—Cricket's sleek body.

A cup of coffee
to wake with, for a nightcap
two glasses of wine—

you'll find, instead of the silence
you were after, oblivion

likc the flood waters,
muddy and thick, making of homes
islanded houses.

Here, a spring-blue sky above
Walden Pond all aglitter.

Into the water
they waded. Footprints on
the path disappearing . . .

At trail's edge, a red-spotted
purple emerges, turns back.

This year, for the second
time in equal measure, daylight
clear and cool, clear night.

Like the Head Chef's, one noted his
style in the embellishments.

What lingers—not
the elaborate garden, but
the dead black squirrel's hands.

Trucks rumbled past the white tent;
words flowed with the stop-and-go.

She unfolded chairs
unconvinced that if you
billed it, they would come.

Come what may, the talk kept on
constant as lake water lapping.

Overhead, churning
in a darkening sky, sea
gulls like whirligigs,

like the wind's gathering strength—
suddenly vanished.

x.

In the stone circle
at Bright Hill Farm, a light breeze
brushes, lifts this hand

as, up ahead, Luke's tail skirts
the corn stubble's open ground.

When the lights were dimmed
in the auditorium,
her face—the one moon;

her eyes, stones for a moment
as the car sped on in the storm.

Baker Farm seems so
desolate after a week
on the road. Air chilled,

not one bird. But still, listening—
alone to shake off the dust

of travel. The cat
stroking doorway, counter's corners,
ankle, open hand—

will undo each angled edge
with its own sleek precisions.

When you enter that
place, trees, the body, yours and
not yours, are one breath,

inhaled by the wind be-
fore squirrel squawk, small bird chatter,

the particular
sound rain makes against leaves—
and are glad to be here.

Bare branches, whispers, green shade—
and now, trees in their showy dress.

Oh, Margaret, how ride
this moment to its crest if
heat didn't recede?

Crumbling under turning wheels
brown leaves, a few yellow leaves,

but from this high window,
blue, a dazzle of trees,
a drizzle of leaves.

"I'm putting on my top hat,"
and, dear heart, walking the talk.

Struck in the same spot
over and over—the fixed
target. So, you move

and in moving are moved toward
a clarifying stillness

then away again.
It's all a balancing act:
snow, showers, drought, frost—

or call it endless cycles
of waxing and waning heat.

Wherever it is,
Cricket finds the warmest spot
to stretch, full length, in.

Did it mark the sparrow's flight—
this squirrel raiding the feeder?

Striking out alone—
lost on a poorly marked trail
headed back toward home.

Red balloons topped with silly
yellow caps—these bittersweets.

No elevator—
and so two flights up we must
ascend stair by stair.

There, in the understory,
trees uprooted, branches snapped—

releasing the hand
that led you there, you finger
these books laid open.

The woods are reclaiming stones
piled into walls long ago;

on fallen white pines,
fungi like dull cousins of
silvery fish scales.

In a clearing, the wind stirs,
catches a leaf, brown and brittle,

that's curved like a sail
till the wind lets go, lets fall,
till the wind lets go.

xi.

Dangling like earrings—
the honey locust's brown pods
now easy to see.

Inspiring but also sad,
the aging star quarterback.

Wind and rain break loose
leaves readied for letting go.
Branches flex. Roots hold.

In the Atlantic, fragments
of EgyptAir Flight 990.

Late afternoon light
sets aflame the remaining
still yellowing trees.

Repeatedly calling till
silence responds to silence.

She stoops to pick up
the cone of a hemlock that
flowers in her hand.

On the city sidewalk coins
we do not stop to pick up.

You know, "When in Rome"—
so at Half Moon Bay it's a
casual affair.

At Francis Beach, pelicans,
boardless surfers, skim the waves.

For the moment, our-
selves sated, we watch sandpipers,
open-billed, probing.

Caught in the swim of traffic
we turn on the radio

and sing to oldies
punctuated by brake lights
down Route 92.

What sustains us is always
and is near—we wake and sleep,

come home to apples,
the season's last tomatoes,
a sprinkle of snow.

Rough waters off Cape Cod bite
several species of sea turtles.

Leonid showers
above clouds, artificial
lights, and us—unseen.

As if each muscle, nerve, cell
flared, that moment, it was like . . .

In a single wave
the blackbirds sweep upward, leave
then unleave the tree—

a picture distance affords—
dots freckling a pastel sky.

Sometimes one plus one
is one—as when, say, man and
woman, one blackbird.

Say bon voyage, adios,
zaìjiàn, ja matta, ah-tchoo!

Karumi—beyond
sabi, it's what Bashō sought—
sheer transparency,

self's veil lifted: to be seen
through, like a struck bell sounding.

On that verge, we are
one voice, one body, the one
steady rain falling.

"Keep your shirt on," she says,
unfolding an umbrella.

The anxious young cook
hopes dumpling-size lumps will stir
down to smooth gravy.

Meanwhile, her mother scrapes with
a blade the measuring cup's rim.

It's a mystery, this
cool blue day nearing the sea-
son's, the century's, end.

The leaves having fallen, sunlight
filters down to a hawk, walking.

xii.

When the tide rolls out
we remember the sight of
waves breaking offshore.

Listen: *out of the cradle
endlessly rocking*, the sea.

Outside the window
near the table where you write,
titmouse, chickadee.

Can it be? Thirty years e-
rased by a fire in Worcester.

We surveyed the ruins—
metal lockers like candles,
gone, our paper lives.

Having anchored the third
strand, a spider is weaving.

"Like sneezing," Master
Jou said, "It's all mind." Body
answers, eyes closed.

"Making it," we used to say:
quick escape from a stuck place.

In the dream of fire
only the scaffolding burns.
But in Worcester,

stretching three miles, fifteen thou-
sand; inside mourning, yet more.

Even buffeted
by these icy winds, to be
outside is worthwhile.

What is there to know? We learn,
love, by going where to go.

No child to suckle,
her breasts ached. Milk. Nothing to
do but express it.

"Spirit road," he calls the spine
stretched between heaven and earth.

We, whose bodies are
lakes, want the fluency of
salt wash sweeping sand,

sand sifting grain by grain through
the thin waist of the hourglass.

As nights lengthen, our
lips release puffs of breath grown
visible, like smoke.

Cold weather fireflies—those
lit ends of their cigarettes.

Instead of the words
"I do," why not say, "You bet"
to even the odds.

Even in freeze, at the core
of the compost heap, some warmth.

On the threshold of
winter, our chafed hands wanted
a dab of rose milk.

Moonlit, an old white-gold ring
on this, the darkest evening.

A ripening peach
it was, rising, the moon out-
facing city lights.

Mudslides. At sea, oil spills torched,
fused wires, an axe's dull head.

Clean edges of salt
crystals dissolve in a whirl
of lukewarm water.

Gazing far, far down the road
where the wooden bridge collapsed.

White pond lilies
summered over murky
water now frozen,

where below fish and frog sleep.
This month's only snow is dust.

She moves in darkness
as that darkness moves, earthbound,
an echo of waves,

broken at first light. The sun
dreams us awake, day by day.

And so whatever
it is, let it come, come rain
or sunshine, come even snow.

Acknowledgments

Some of these poems, a few in slightly different versions or under different titles, first appeared in the following publications:

Crab Orchard Review: "The Eulogy," "Taproot";
Kestrel: "Adam's Apple," "Hail," Section iii (March) of "Patchwork of Selvage," "Soap," "Strays";
North Carolina Literary Review: "Customs," " 'Crazy' ";
North Dakota Quarterly: Section v (May) of "Patchwork of Selvage";
The Southern Review: "Ordinary Moons."

"Arrival" was first published in *Urban Nature: Poems about Wildlife in the City* (Milkweed Editions, 2000).

"Taproot" also appeared in *The Best American Poetry* (Scribners, 1999) and *News of Home* (BOA Editions, 1998).

"Hail" is for Betty Adcock; "Ordinary Moons" is for Peter Makuck; and Section v (May) of "Patchwork of Selvage" is for Patricia Goedicke.

My gratitude to the following individuals: Tadashi "Shōkan" Kondo for lessons in link-and-shift techniques during several renku-writing sessions and during informal conversations that unfolded between the fall of 1998 and the spring of 2000; Sarah Freligh, whose playful note, "Rengay on, boogie woman," arrived at exactly the moment I needed to hear it; Scot Miller for the memory of Beech Spring before the backhoe & Marilyn Miller for her impeccable eye; Suzanne Owens & bg Thurston for nourishment in its many forms; LaoMa & the late Jou, Tsung Hwa, for lessons in daily practice; Thom Ward, Steve Huff, & Sarah Daniels at BOA Editions for their enthusiastic support of this experiment; Richard Foerster for help fixing it; David Dean & Jessica Mirch, weathering the difficult year, and my husband Bradley P. Dean, to whom this book is dedicated—*auwē*!

About the Author

Debra Kang Dean is the author of *News of Home* (BOA Editions, 1998), which co-won the Sheila Margaret Motton Award, sponsored by the New England Poetry Club; and *Back to Back*, which won the 1997 Harperprints Poetry Chapbook Competition, judged by Ruth Stone. Her poems have appeared in a number of anthologies, including *The Best American Poetry*, *The New American Poets: A Bread Loaf Anthology*, and *Yobo: Korean American Writing in Hawai'i*.

A senior student in the Magic Tortoise Taijiquan School in Chapel Hill, North Carolina, she teaches taiji in Peterborough, New Hampshire. She is also a contributing editor for *Tar River Poetry* and teaches poetry online at the UCLA Extension Writers' Program. She works in customer service and lives in West Peterborough with her husband Brad, and Bashō and Cricket, their two cats.

✦

BOA EDITIONS, LTD.

AMERICAN POETS CONTINUUM SERIES

No. 1 *The Fuhrer Bunker: A Cycle of Poems in Progress*
W. D. Snodgrass

No. 2 *She*
M. L. Rosenthal

No. 3 *Living With Distance*
Ralph J. Mills, Jr.

No. 4 *Not Just Any Death*
Michael Waters

No. 5 *That Was Then: New and Selected Poems*
Isabella Gardner

No. 6 *Things That Happen Where There Aren't Any People*
William Stafford

No. 7 *The Bridge of Change: Poems 1974–1980*
John Logan

No. 8 *Signatures*
Joseph Stroud

No. 9 *People Live Here: Selected Poems 1949–1983*
Louis Simpson

No. 10 *Yin*
Carolyn Kizer

No. 11 *Duhamel: Ideas of Order in Little Canada*
Bill Tremblay

No. 12 *Seeing It Was So*
Anthony Piccione

No. 13 *Hyam Plutzik: The Collected Poems*

No. 14 *Good Woman: Poems and a Memoir 1969–1980*
Lucille Clifton

No. 15 *Next: New Poems*
Lucille Clifton

No. 16 *Roxa: Voices of the Culver Family*
William B. Patrick

No. 17 *John Logan: The Collected Poems*

No. 18 *Isabella Gardner: The Collected Poems*

No. 19 *The Sunken Lightship*
Peter Makuck

No. 20 *The City in Which I Love You*
Li-Young Lee

No. 21 *Quilting: Poems 1987–1990*
Lucille Clifton

No. 22 *John Logan: The Collected Fiction*

No. 23 *Shenandoah and Other Verse Plays*
Delmore Schwartz

No. 24 *Nobody Lives on Arthur Godfrey Boulevard*
Gerald Costanzo

No. 25 *The Book of Names: New and Selected Poems*
Barton Sutter

No. 26 *Each in His Season*
W. D. Snodgrass

No. 27 *Wordworks: Poems Selected and New*
Richard Kostelanetz

No. 28 *What We Carry*
Dorianne Laux

No. 29 *Red Suitcase*
Naomi Shihab Nye

No. 30 *Song*
Brigit Pegeen Kelly

No. 31 *The Fuehrer Bunker: The Complete Cycle*
W. D. Snodgrass

No. 32 *For the Kingdom*
Anthony Piccione

No. 33 *The Quicken Tree*
Bill Knott

No. 34 *These Upraised Hands*
William B. Patrick

No. 35 *Crazy Horse in Stillness*
William Heyen

No. 36 *Quick, Now, Always*
Mark Irwin

Bing

Colophon

Precipitates, Poems by Debra Kang Dean,
was set by Richard Foerster, York Beach, Maine,
using Monotype Dante with Rococo Ornaments.
The cover was designed by Lisa Mauro / Mauro Design,
with a photograph by Scot Miller.
Manufacturing was by McNaughton & Gunn, Saline, Michigan.

→>-<←

The publication of this book was made possible in part by the special
support of the following individuals:

Deborah Smith-Bernstein & Martin B. Bernstein
Ida Mae Arrand-Dean   →>-<←   Nelson Blish
Nancy & Alan Cameros
David P. K. Dean & Bradley P. Dean
Dr. Henry & Beverly French   →>-<←   David B. Ganoe
Robert & Adele Gardner
Suzanne & Gerard Gouvernet
Kip & Deb Hale
Peter & Robin Hursh   →>-<←   Robert & Willy Hursh
Richard Garth & Mimi Hwang
Dane & Judy Gordon
Marge & Don Grinols
William Hauser
Holly Mathews & Ron Hoag
Louise Klinke   →>-<←   Marilyn & Scot Miller
Robert & Sharon Napier
Boo Poulin
James Robie & Edith Matthai
Deborah Ronnen
Andrea & Paul Rubery
Jane Schuster   →>-<←   Sue Stewart
Judith Taylor
Pat & Michael Wilder